THE KNITTED
NURSERY COLLECTION

14 cuddly toys and colourful accessories for babies

Jem Weston

Published in 2016 by
Search Press Ltd
Wellwood
North Farm Road
Tunbridge Wells
Kent, TN2 3DR
UK

ISBN: 978-1-78221-317-8

Conceived, designed and produced by
Quail Publishing
2/3 Black Horse Barns
Fancott
Toddington
Bedfordshire, LU5 6HT
UK

Art Editor: Georgina Brant
Graphic Design: Quail Studio
Technical Editor: Marilyn Wilson
Photography: Jesse Wild
Creative Director: Darren Brant
Yarn Support: Rowan Yarns
Designer: Jem Weston

Printed in China

NOTE:
Rowan Yarns can be substituted
by any yarn of similar weight.

THE KNITTED
NURSERY COLLECTION

14 cuddly toys and colourful accessories for babies

Jem Weston

SEARCH PRESS

CONTENTS

ABOUT JEM WESTON

Jem Weston is a freelance designer, author and workshop tutor with a passion for colour and craft.

Jem's affection for knitting began at a young age when she was taught to knit by her Grandma. It grew into an addiction during her time at university where she studied Fine Art, focusing on sculpture and installation, often inspired by traditional crafts.

Having worked closely with Coats Crafts and Rowan Yarns since 2008, as the Rowan Design Consultant Manager and Coats Crafts Territory Manager, Jem is now a freelance Rowan Workshop Tutor.

Jem currently lives in Nottingham and is dedicated to passing on knitting skills through inspiring workshops and design.

PROJECTS

BERTIE
AND BEA
BUNNIES

page 12

BERTIE
AND BEA
QUILTS

page 20

FELTED
TOY
BASKET

page 30

FLOCK
PILLOW

page 34

FLOCK
WALL
HANGING

page 38

FLUTTERBY
FLOOR
PILLOW

page 42

FLUTTERBIES

page 46

GINGER
SQUIRREL

page 50

GINGER
BLANKET

page 58

POM POM
BUNTING

page 66

SLEEPY
OWL
PILLOW

page 70

OLLIE AND
POLLY
ELEPHANT

page 76

OLLIE AND
POLLY
BLANKETS

page 84

CIRCULAR
FELTED
RUG

page 88

BERTIE AND
BEA BUNNIES

Bertie and Bea are soft and cuddly happy bunnies.
Their fluffy pom pom tails and fabric ears add colour and
texture for your little one.

MATERIALS

YARN

Rowan Baby Merino Silk DK

	Bea	Bertie	
A	Dawn 672	Dawn 672	2 × 50g
B	Claret 700	Iceberg 699	1 × 50g

FABRIC

Bea: 25 × 25cm (10 × 10in) piece of Denyse Schmidt, Zig Zag Dash in glade, cut to size using pinking shears

Bertie: 25 × 25cm (10 × 10in) piece of Parson Gray, Wind Arrows in slate, cut to size using pinking shears

NEEDLES

1 pair 3.75mm (no 9) (US 5) needles

EXTRAS

Washable toy stuffing

65mm (2½in) pom pom maker
Oddment of dark grey yarn

TENSION

23 sts and 32 rows to 10cm (4in) measured over st st using 3.75mm (US 5) needles.

FINISHED SIZE

Completed bunny measures approx. 26cm (10¼in) tall, 15cm (6in) wide and 14cm (5½in) deep.

FRONT SECTION

Using 3.75mm (US 5) needles and yarn A cast on 6 sts.

BASE

Row 1 Knit.
Row 2 Purl.
Row 3 K1, M1, K to last st, M1, K1. *8 sts*
Row 4 Purl.
Row 5 K1, M1, K to last st, M1, K1. *10 sts*
Row 6 Purl.
Row 7 K1, M1, K to last st, M1, K1. *12 sts*
Beg with P row, work 11 rows in st st.
Next row K1, K2tog tbl, K to last 3 sts, K2tog, K1. *10 sts*
Beg with P row, work 3 rows in st st.
Next row K1, K2tog tbl, K to last 3 sts, K2tog, K1. *8 sts*
Next row Purl.

FEET

Cast on 18 sts at beg of next 2 rows. *44 sts*
Next row K1, M1, K16, K2tog tbl, K6, K2tog, K16, M1, K1. *44 sts*
Next row Purl.
Next row K18, K2tog tbl, K4, K2tog, K18. *42 sts*
Next row Purl.
Next row K18, K2tog tbl, K2, K2tog, K18. *40 sts*
Beg with P row, work 5 rows in st st.
Next row K1, K2tog tbl, K to last 3 sts, K2tog, K1. *38 sts*
Next row Purl.
Next row K1, K2tog tbl, K to last 3 sts, K2tog, K1. *36 sts*
Next row Purl.

LEGS

Cast off 7 sts at beg of next 2 rows. *22 sts*
Beg with K row, work 12 rows in st st.
Next row K1, K2tog tbl, K to last 3 sts, K2tog, K1. *20 sts*
Beg with P row, work 3 rows in st st.
Next row K1, K2tog tbl, K to last 3 sts, K2tog, K1. *18 sts*
Next row Purl.
Next row K1, K2tog tbl, K5, M1, K2, M1, K5, K2tog, K1. *18 sts*
Next row Purl.
Next row K1, K2tog tbl, K4, M1, K4, M1, K4, K2tog, K1. *18 sts*
Next row Purl.
Cast off 4 sts at beg of next 2 rows. *10 sts*

TUMMY

Beg with K row, work 6 rows in st st.

ARMS

Cast on 10 sts at beg of next 2 rows. *30 sts*
Next row K1, M1, K9, M1, K10, M1, K9, M1, K1. *34 sts*
Next row Purl.
Next row K1, M1, K11, M1, K10, M1, K11, M1, K1. *38 sts*
Next row Purl.
Next row K14, M1, K10, M1, K14. *40 sts*
Next row Purl.
Next row K15, M1, K10, M1, K15. *42 sts*
Next row Purl.
Next row K16, M1, K10, M1, K16. *44 sts*
Next row Purl.
Next row K1, K2tog tbl, K14, M1, K10, M1, K14, K2tog, K1. *44 sts*
Next row Purl.
Next row K1, K2tog tbl, K14, M1, K10, M1, K14, K2tog, K1. *44 sts*
Next row Purl.
Cast off 18 sts at beg of next 2 rows. *8 sts*

NECK/CHIN

Beg with K row, work 8 rows in st st.
Next row K1, K2tog tbl, K to last 3 sts, K2tog, K1. *6 sts*
Beg with P row, work 5 rows in st st.
Next row K1, K2tog tbl, K2tog, K1. *4 sts*
Next row Purl.
Cast off.

BACK SECTION

Using 3.75mm (US 5) needles and yarn A cast on 68 sts. Place marker on 18th st from each edge to denote the back of feet.

FEET

Next row K1, M1, K25, M1, K16, M1, K25, M1, K1. *72 sts*
Next row Purl.
Next row K27, M1, K18, M1, K27. *74 sts*
Beg with P row, work 7 rows in st st.

Next row K1, K2tog tbl, K25, M1, K18, M1, K25, K2tog, K1. *74 sts*
Next row Purl.
Next row K1, K2tog tbl, K to last 3 sts, K2tog, K1. *72 sts*
Next row Purl.

LEGS
Cast off 7 sts at beg of next 2 rows. *58 sts*
Next row K20, M1, K18, M1, K20. *60 sts*
Beg with P row, work 11 rows in st st.
Next row K1, K2tog tbl, K to last 3 sts, K2tog, K1. *58 sts*
Beg with P row, work 3 rows in st st.
Next row K1, K2tog tbl, K to last 3 sts, K2tog, K1. *56 sts*
Next row Purl.
Next row K1, K2tog tbl, K to last 3 sts, K2tog, K1. *54 sts*
Next row Purl.
Next row K1, K2tog tbl, K to last 3 sts, K2tog, K1. *52 sts*
Next row Purl.
Cast off 5 sts at beg of next 2 rows. *42 sts*

BACK
Next row K10, K2tog tbl, K18, K2tog, K10. *40 sts*
Next row Purl.
Next row K10, K2tog tbl, K16, K2tog, K10. *38 sts*
Beg with P row, work 3 rows in st st.

ARMS
Cast on 10 sts at beg of next 2 rows. *58 sts*
Next row K1, M1, K9, M1, K10, K2tog tbl, K14, K2tog, K10, M1, K9, M1, K1. *60 sts*
Next row Purl.
Next row K1, M1, K11, M1, K36, M1, K11, M1, K1. *64 sts*
Next row Purl.
Next row K14, M1, K36, M1, K14. *66 sts*
Next row Purl.
Next row K15, M1, K10, K2tog tbl, K12, K2tog, K10, M1, K15. *66 sts*
Next row Purl.
Next row K16, M1, K34, M1, K16. *68 sts*
Next row Purl.
Next row K1, K2tog tbl, K14, M1, K34, M1, K14, K2tog, K1. *68 sts*
Next row Purl.
Next row K1, K2tog tbl, K14, M1, K10, K2tog tbl, K10, K2tog, K10, M1, K14, K2tog, K1. *66 sts*
Next row Purl.
Cast off 18 sts at beg of next 2 rows. *30 sts*

HEAD
Cast on 12 sts at beg of next 2 rows. *54 sts*
Next row K21, K2tog tbl, K8, K2tog, K21. *52 sts*
Next row Purl.
Next row K20, K2tog tbl, K8, K2tog, K20. *50 sts*
Next row Purl.
Next row K1, K2tog tbl, K18, M1, K8, M1, K18, K2tog, K1. *50 sts*
Beg with P row, work 3 rows in st st.
Next row K1, K2tog tbl, K18, M1, K8, M1, K18, K2tog, K1. *50 sts*
Beg with P row, work 3 rows in st st.
Next row K1, K2tog tbl, K to last 3 sts, K2tog, K1. *48 sts*
Beg with P row, work 3 rows in st st.
Next row K1, K2tog tbl, K to last 3 sts, K2tog, K1. *46 sts*
Next row Purl.
Cast off 17 sts at beg of next 2 rows. *12 sts*
Next row K1, M1, K to last st, M1, K1. *14 sts*
Beg with P row, work 3 rows in st st.

Next row K1, M1, K to last st, M1, K1. *16 sts*
Beg with P row, work 19 rows in st st.
Place marker at each end of last row to
denote beg of face shaping.
Next row K1, K2tog tbl, K to last 3 sts,
K2tog, K1. *14 sts*
Beg with P row, work 3 rows in st st.
Next row K1, K2tog tbl, K to last 3 sts,
K2tog, K1. *12 sts*
Beg with P row, work 3 rows in st st.
Next row K1, K2tog tbl, K to last 3 sts,
K2tog, K1. *10 sts*
Beg with P row, work 3 rows in st st.
Next row K1, K2tog tbl, K to last 3 sts,
K2tog, K1. *8 sts*
Beg with P row, work 3 rows in st st.
Next row K1, K2tog tbl, K to last 3 sts,
K2tog, K1. *6 sts*
Beg with P row, work 3 rows in st st.
Next row K1, K2tog tbl, K to last 3 sts,
K2tog, K1. *4 sts*
Next row Purl.
Cast off.

EARS (BOTH ALIKE)
Using 3.75mm (US 5) needles and yarn A
cast on 6 sts.

Row 1 K1, M1, K to last st, M1, K1. *8 sts*
Row 2 Purl.
Work in st st. Inc as set by row 1 on next,
1 foll alt row and 3 foll 4th rows. *18 sts*
Beg with P row, work 5 rows in st st.
Next row K1, K2tog tbl, K to last 3 sts,
K2tog, K1. *16 sts*
Dec as set on 4 foll 4th rows. *8 sts*
Beg with P row, work 3 rows in st st.
Cast off.

POM POM TAIL
Using yarn B and 65mm (2½in) pom pom
maker – make a pom pom.

MAKING UP

Using mattress stitch, join top section of head to sides of head, with face section (from markers), sewn along edges of side sections.

Matching arms, legs and markers on back section to back of feet on front section – join front and back sections, leaving base open.

Stuff the toy firmly.

Join base evenly along cast on edge of back section.

Using dark grey yarn, embroider eyes and nose on face.

Sew pom pom tail firmly in position.

Pin ears to fabric and cut fabric to shape using pinking shears. Sew fabric ear lining to knitted ears and steam/block flat.

Sew cast off edge of ears in position on head, using image as a guide.

BERTIE AND BEA QUILTS

These cosy quilts combine knitting and fabric and coordinate beautifully with the Bertie and Bea Bunnies. You can choose from a pink or blue colourway.

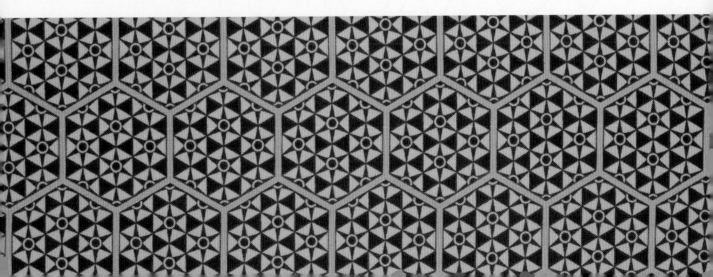

MATERIALS

YARN
Rowan Baby Merino Silk DK

BERTIE
A	Dawn	672	2 x 50g
B	Zinc	681	2 x 50g
C	Iceberg	699	1 x 50g
D	Emerald	685	1 x 50g

BEA
A	Dawn	672	2 x 50g
B	Zinc	681	2 x 50g
C	Rose	678	1 x 50g
D	Claret	700	1 x 50g

NEEDLES
1 pair 4mm (no 8) (US 6) needles

EXTRAS
84 x 84cm (33 x 30in) piece of
2oz (75g) wadding/batting

FABRIC
Please note: All fabric pieces must be cut to size with pinking shears/overlocked or zigzag stitched to avoid fraying. Knitted squares should measure 20cm (8in) – if they are larger or smaller, please adjust fabric sizes accordingly.

BERTIE
Parson Gray Shaman collection;
1 Peyote Moon, cloud 2 x 24 x 24cm (9½ x 9½in) pieces, cut to size using pinking shears.

2 Celestial, moon 2 x 24 x 24cm (9½ x 9½in) pieces, cut to size using pinking shears.

3 Hopi, blank 2 x 24 x 24cm (9½ x 9½in) pieces plus 1 x 92 x 92cm (36¼ x 36¼in) piece for backing, cut to size using pinking shears.

4 Wind Arrows, slate 2 x 24 x 24cm (9½ x 9½in) pieces, cut to size using pinking shears.

BEA

Denyse Schmidt Franklin collection;

1 Circle Squares, glade 2 × 24 × 24cm (9½ × 9½in) pieces, cut to size using pinking shears.

2 Zigzag Dash, glade 2 × 24 × 24cm (9½ × 9½in) pieces, cut to size using pinking shears.

3 Curly Cues, glade 2 × 24 × 24cm (9½ × 9½in) pieces, cut to size using pinking shears.

4 Windowpane Panel, glade 2 × 24 × 24cm (9½ × 9½in) pieces plus 1 × 92 × 92cm (36¼ × 36¼in) piece for backing, cut to size using pinking shears.

TENSION
22 sts and 30 rows to 10cm (4in) measured over st st using 4mm (US 6) needles.

FINISHED SIZE
Finished quilt measures approx. 84cm (33in) square.

SQUARE A (MAKE 2)
Using yarn A and 4mm (US 6) needles cast on 46 sts.

Working in st st throughout, starting with a K row and using the intarsia technique, complete chart A (page 25).
Cast off.

SQUARE B (MAKE 2)
Using yarn D and 4mm (US 6) needles cast on 46 sts.

Working in st st throughout, starting with a K row and using the intarsia technique, complete chart B (page 26).
Cast off.

SQUARE C (MAKE 2)
Using yarn C and 4mm (US 6) needles cast on 46 sts.

Working in st st throughout, starting with a K row and using the intarsia technique, complete chart C (page 27).
Cast off.

SQUARE D (MAKE 2)
Using yarn B and 4mm (US 6) needles cast on 46 sts.

Working in st st throughout, starting with a K row and using the intarsia technique, complete chart D (page 28).
Cast off.

MAKING UP

Iron a crease 2cm(¾in) in from the edge of each fabric square to create a guide line for sewing together.

With RS of knitting facing RS of fabric, handsew the knitted and fabric squares together following the making up plan and sewing along creased lines on fabric.

Iron under 1.5cm (½in) seam allowance along all 4 edges of backing fabric (this will fold over to create the edge around the quilt top).

Using a fabric pencil, mark 7.5cm (3in) from each corner in both directions. Fold fabric diagonally, with RS of fabric facing each other and sew along line from centre to seam allowance – leaving seam allowance unstitched to turn under.

Turn RS out, folding excess fabric into corner and press flat. Repeat this for each corner.

Lay out quilt back with WS facing, lay wadding/batting on top and then quilt top with RS facing. Fold edges of backing over all layers and pin in position.

Machine or handsew close to edge of quilt edging, with 1.5cm (½in) seam allowance tucked inwards and ensuring you are catching all layers.

Secure all three layers in place by handstitching 2 small stitches through all layers where corners of squares meet.

MAKING UP PLAN

B	3	C	4
1	A	2	D
C	4	B	3
2	D	1	A

CHART A

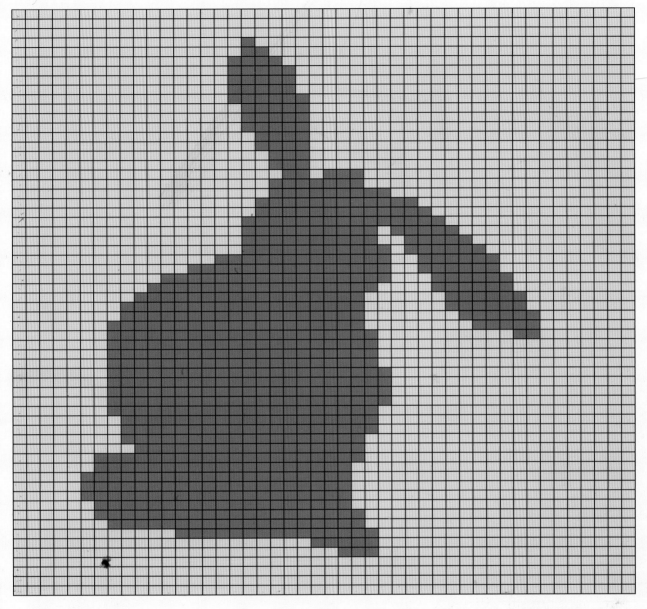

ROW I

KEY

 Yarn A

Yarn B

CHART B

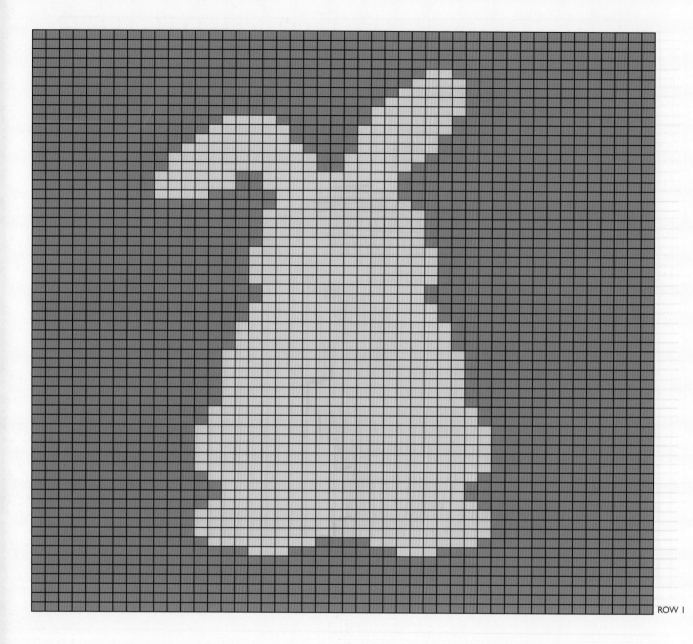

ROW 1

KEY

 Yarn D

Yarn A

CHART C

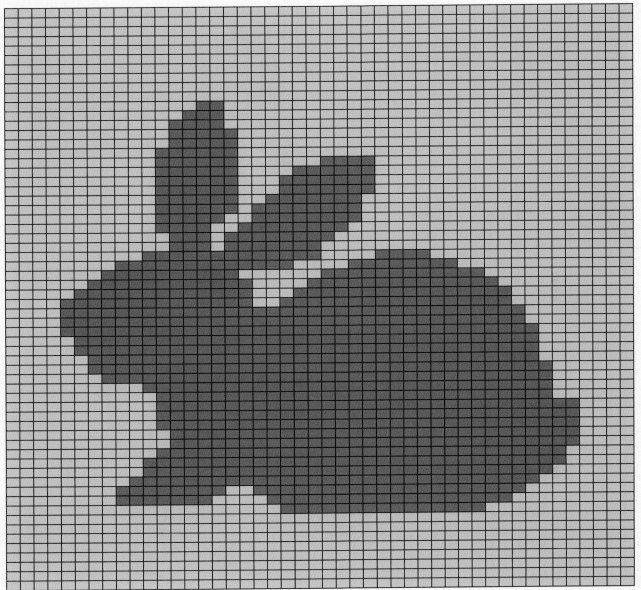

ROW 1

KEY

 Yarn B

☐ Yarn C

CHART D

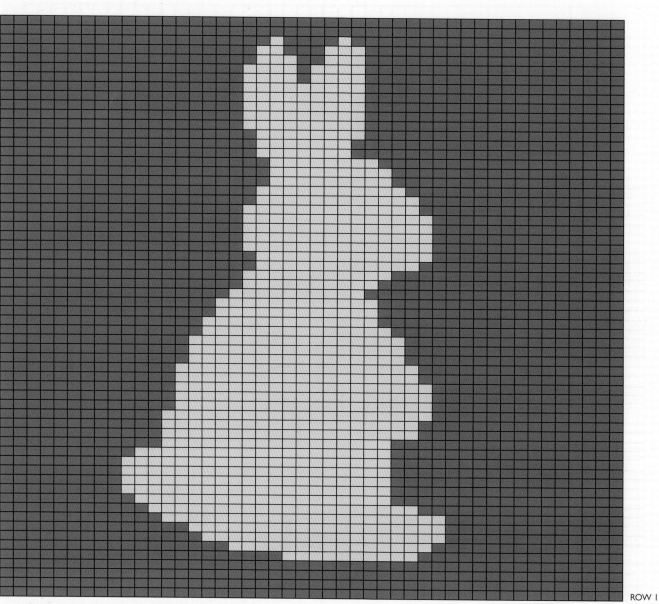

ROW I

KEY

 Yarn B

 Yarn A

28

FELTED
TOY BASKET

This toy basket is perfect for keeping all your newly knitted toys neat and tidy. The simple basket is knitted and then felted in the washing machine.

MATERIALS

YARN

Rowan Creative Focus Worsted

| A | Nickel | 00401 | 2 x 100g |
| B | Saffron | 03810 | 2 x 100g |

NEEDLES

1 pair 4.5mm (no 7) (US 7) circular needle

EXTRAS

Sewing thread
Seam ripper
Tweezers
Box or stiff card

TENSION

Before felting: 19 sts and 39 rows to 10cm (4in) measured over garter st and 20 sts and 25 rows measured over st st using 4.5mm (US 7) needles.

After felting: 27.5 sts and 60 rows to 10cm (4in) measured over garter st and 26 sts and 40 rows measured over st st using 4.5mm (US 7) needles.

FINISHED SIZE

Completed basket measures approx. 27cm (10⅝in) wide, 27cm (10⅝in) deep and 20cm (7⅞in) tall.

TOY BASKET

Using yarn A and 4.5mm (US 7) needle cast on 75 sts.

Working back and forth across these 75 sts, work 150 rows g st.
With WS facing, pick up and Knit 75 sts along right edge of base, 75 sts along cast on edge and 75 sts along left side of base.
300 sts
Place marker on 1st stitch and now start working in the round.
Change to yarn B

Round 1 Knit.
Round 2 Knit.
Change to yarn A
Round 3 Knit.
Round 4 Knit.
These 4 rounds form patt.
Cont in patt for a further 40 rounds, ending after round 4.
Change to yarn B and cont in st st for 26 rounds.
Next round K100, cast of 25 sts (1 st on right needle), K124, cast off 25 sts, K to end.
Change to yarn A
Next round K100, cast on 25 sts, K125, cast on 25 sts, K to end.
Change to yarn B
Cont in st st for 8 rounds.
Next round *K1, P1, rep from * to end.
Next round *K1, P1, rep from * to end.
Cast off.

MAKING UP
Block top edge of basket flat.

Loosely stitch handle holes closed using sewing thread (to be removed after felting).

Wash on its own at 40°C.

Please note, washing machines vary so it is important to felt a test swatch to check the shrinkage before felting your basket. Do not use a delicate cycle.

Washing at 40°C will create a thick felt and the toy basket will need to be shaped to size straight after washing, while damp.

Carefully unpick handle holes using a seam ripper and remove any stray thread with tweezers.

Cut a box or stiff card to required size and pin felted basket to size/shape over box.

FLOCK PILLOW

This pillow, with its flock of colourful birds, is perfect for adding some colour and extra comfort to your nursing chair.

MATERIALS

YARN

Rowan Pure Wool Superwash DK

A	Shale	002	3 x 50g
B	Anthracite	003	1 x 50g
C	Raspberry	028	1 x 50g
D	Avocado	019	1 x 50g
E	Gold	051	1 x 50g

FABRIC

29 x 50cm (11½ x 19¾in) piece of Tula Pink Chain Mail fabric in tartx, cut to size using pinking shears

40 x 50cm (16 x 19¾in) piece of Tula Pink Chain Mail fabric in tartx, cut to size using pinking shears

NEEDLES

1 pair 4mm (no 8) (US 6) needles

EXTRAS

46cm (18in) square pillow pad

TENSION

22 sts and 30 rows to 10cm (4in) measured over st st using 4mm (US 6) needles

FINISHED SIZE

Knitted pillow panel measures approx. 46cm (18in) square.

FRONT

Using yarn A and 4mm (US 6) needles, cast on 103 sts.

Working in st st throughout, starting with a K row and using the intarsia technique, complete chart (page 37).
Cast off.

MAKING UP

Pillow cover back: For opening edges, turn under 2cm (¾in) along one long edge of each piece. Turn under again and straight stitch in place. With RS of knitting facing RS of fabric, place smaller piece on the knitted front first, place the larger piece on top, overlapping in the middle. Pin and handstitch the sides of the two pieces to the knitted front.

Turn the right sides out and insert pillow pad.

KEY

Yarn A
Yarn B
Yarn C
Yarn D
Yarn E

FLOCK WALL HANGING

Brighten up your nursery walls with this resting flock of rainbow birds. Great on their own or with the Flock Pillow.

MATERIALS

YARN

Rowan Cotton Glace

A	Winsor	849	1 x 50g
B	Shoot	814	1 x 50g
C	Persimmon	832	1 x 50g
D	Poppy	741	1 x 50g
E	Lipstick	865	1 x 50g
F	Mineral	856	1 x 50g

NEEDLES

1 pair 3.25mm (no 10) (US 3) needles

EXTRAS

Washable toy stuffing

A twig between 35cm (13¾in) and 70cm (27½in)

Approx. 1m x 3mm (39 x ⅛in) double satin pale grey ribbon

TENSION

23 sts and 32 rows to 10cm (4in) measured over st st using 3.25mm (US 3) needles.

FINISHED SIZE

Each bird measures approx. 16cm (6¼in) tall including tail, 4cm (1½in) wide and 4cm (1½in) deep.

BIRDS
BACK (MAKE 1 OF EACH IN YARNS A, B, C, D AND E)

Using yarn A, B, C, D or E and 3.25mm (US 3) needles, cast on 3 sts.

Work in g st for 14 rows.
Next row K1, M1, K to last st, M1, K1. *5 sts*
Cont in g st for 13 rows.
Next row K1, M1, K to last st, M1, K1. *7 sts*
Next row Purl.
Work in st st. Inc as set on next, 4 foll alt rows and 3 foll 4th rows. *23 sts*
Beg with P row, work 5 rows st st.
Next row K1, SSK, K to last 3 sts, K2tog, K1. *21 sts*
This row sets dec.
Dec as set on 3 foll alt rows. *15 sts*

Place a marker at each end of next row to denote start of head.
Next row Purl.
Next row K1, M1, K to last st, M1, K1. *17 sts*
Beg with P row, work 5 rows st st.
Next row K5, SSK, K3, K2tog, K5. *15 sts*
Next row Purl.
Next row K4, SSK, K3, K2tog, K4. *13 sts*
Next row Purl.
Next row K3, SSK, K3, K2tog, K3. *11 sts*
Next row Purl.
Next row K2, SSK, K3, K2tog, K2. *9 sts*
Next row Purl.
Next row K1, SSK, K3, K2tog, K1. *7 sts*
Next row Purl.
Change to yarn F for beak
Next row SSK, K3, K2tog. *5 sts*
Next row Knit.
Next row SSK, K1, K2tog. *3 sts*
Next row Knit.
Next row Sl1, K2tog, PSSO.
Fasten off.

FRONT (MAKE 1 OF EACH IN YARNS A, B, C, D AND E)

Using yarn A, B, C, D or E and 3.25mm (US 3) needles, cast on 5 sts.

Row 1 K1, M1, K to last st, M1, K1. *7 sts*
Beg with P row, work 31 rows st st.
Next row K1, SSK, K to last 3 sts, K2tog, K1. *5 sts*
Place a marker at each end of next row to denote start of chin.
Beg with P row, work 9 rows st st.
Cast off.

MAKING UP

Using mattress st and matching head markers, join front and back sections together between g st tail and beak, stuffing as you go.

Join birds together by threading a strand of yarn through all 5 birds and securing in position on first and last bird.

Attach birds to twig and create feet by stitching through bird and wrapping yarn F around the twig (three times per foot), using the image as a guide.

Tie ribbon to twig, cutting to the required length for hanging.

FLUTTERBY
FLOOR PILLOW

This colourful floor pillow creates great soft seating for your nursery floor and looks lovely with the Flutterbies.

MATERIALS

YARN

Rowan Pure Wool Superwash Worsted

A	Moonstone	112	2 x 100g
B	Mustard	131	1 x 100g
C	Mallard	144	1 x 100g
D	Seville	134	1 x 100g

FABRIC

36.5 x 65cm (14½ x 25½in) piece of Joel Dewberry Tulip fabric in eucalyptus, cut to size using pinking shears

48 x 65cm (19 x 25½in) piece of Joel Dewberry Tulip fabric in eucalyptus, cut to size using pinking shears

NEEDLES

1 pair 4.5mm (no 7) (US 7) needles

EXTRAS

61cm (24in) square pillow pad

TENSION

20 sts and 25 rows to 10cm (4in) measured over st st using 4.5mm (US 7) needles.

FINISHED SIZE

Knitted pillow panel measures approx. 61cm (24in) square.

FRONT

Using yarn A and 4.5mm (US 7) needles cast on 124 sts.

Working in st st throughout, starting with a K row and using the intarsia technique, complete chart (page 45).
Cast off.

MAKING UP

Pillow cover back: For opening edges, turn under 2cm (¾in) along one long edge of each piece. Turn under again and straight stitch in place. With RS of knitting facing RS of fabric, place smaller piece on the knitted front first, place the larger piece on top, overlapping in the middle. Pin and handstitch the sides of the two pieces to the knitted front.

Turn the right sides out and insert pillow pad.

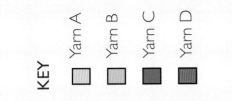

KEY

Yarn A
Yarn B
Yarn C
Yarn D

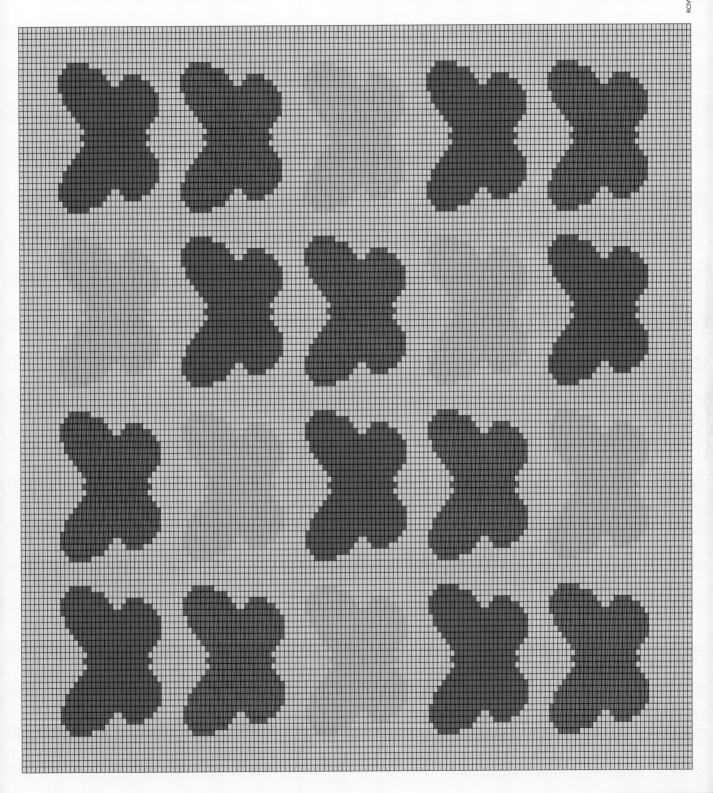

FLUTTERBIES

These simple 'flutterbies' can be hung as decorations,
made into a garland or simply a little soft toy for your
new arrival.

MATERIALS

YARN

Rowan Pure Wool Superwash Worsted

Shown in:

Moonstone	112	1 x 100g
Mustard	131	1 x 100g
Mallard	144	1 x 100g
Seville	134	1 x 100g

NEEDLES

1 pair 4.5mm (no 7) (US 7) needles

EXTRAS

Washable toy stuffing

Approx. 25cm x 3mm (10 x 1/8in) double satin pale grey ribbon for each Flutterby

TENSION

20 sts and 25 rows to 10cm (4in) measured over st st using 4.5mm (US 7) needles.

FINISHED SIZE

Completed flutterbies measure approx. 13cm (5in) wide and 11cm (4½in) tall.

SPECIAL ABBREIVIATIONS

Kfb – Inc 1 st by knitting into the front and back of next st.

FLUTTERFLY FRONT AND BACK (BOTH ALIKE)

Using 4.5mm (US 7) needles cast on 6 sts.

LEFT WING

*Row 1 Knit.
Row 2 P1, M1, P to last st, M1, P1. *8 sts*
Row 3 K1, M1, K to last st, M1, K1. *10 sts*
Beg with P row, work 3 rows in st st.**
Break off yarn and leave on needle.

RIGHT WING

On the same needle, cast on 6 sts and rep from * to **.
Now work across both wings. *20 sts*

Next row Knit.
Next row Purl.
Next row SSK, K to last 2 sts, K2tog. *18 sts*
Next row P2tog, P to last 2 sts, P2tog tbl. *16 sts*
Next row SSK, K to last 2 sts, K2tog. *14 sts*
Next row P2tog, P to last 2 sts, P2tog tbl. *12 sts*
Next row K1, Kfb, K to last 2 sts, Kfb, K1. *14 sts*
Next row P1, M1, P to last st, M1, P1. *16 sts*
Next row K1, M1, K to last st, M1, K1. *18 sts*
Next row P1, M1, P to last st, M1, P1. *20 sts*
Next row K1, M1, K to last st, M1, K1. *22 sts*
Next row Purl.
Next row K1, M1, K to last st, M1, K1. *24 sts*
Next row Purl.
Next row K1, M1, K11 and turn leaving rem
12 sts on holder. *13 sts*
Beg with P row, work 3 rows in st st.
Next row K to last 2 sts, K2tog. *12 sts*
Next row Purl.
Next row K to last 2 sts, K2tog. *11 sts*
Next row P2tog, P to end. 10 sts
Next row K to last 2 sts, K2tog. *9 sts*
Next row P2tog, P to end. 8 sts
Cast off.
Rejoin yarn to 12 sts from holder.

LEFT WING
Next row K to last st, M1, K1. *13 sts*
Beg with P row, work 3 rows in st st.
Next row SSK, K to end. *12 sts*
Next row Purl.
Next row SSK, K to end. *11 sts*
Next row P to last 2 sts, P2tog tbl. *10 sts*
Next row SSK, K to end. *9 sts*
Next row P to last 2 sts, P2tog tbl. *8 sts*
Cast off.

MAKING UP
Place front and back flutterfly pieces together WS facing. Join using mattress st, stuffing as you go.

Using a tapestry needle – thread ribbon through flutterby for hanging, using image as a guide.

GINGER SQUIRREL

Ginger is an adorable tweedy squirrel with a large bushy tail and a simple contrasting scarf – the perfect partner for the Ginger Blanket.

MATERIALS

YARN
Rowan Felted Tweed
A   Ginger 154   2 x 50g

Rowan Kidsilk Haze
B   Blood 627   1 x 50g

Rowan Baby Merino Silk DK
C   Emerald 685   1 x 50g

NEEDLES
1 pair 3.75mm (no 9) (US 5) needles

EXTRAS
Washable toy stuffing
Oddment of dark brown yarn

TENSION
23 sts and 32 rows to 10cm (4in)
measured over st st using 3.75mm (US 5)
needles and yarn A.

20 sts and 44 rows to 10 cm (4in)
measured over g st using 3.75mm (US 5)
needles and yarn A and B held together.

FINISHED SIZE
Completed squirrel measures approx. 26cm
(10¼in) tall, 15cm (6in) wide and
23cm (9in) deep.

FRONT SECTION
Using 3.75mm (US 5) needles and yarns A
and B held together cast on 4 sts.

TAIL
Row 1 Knit.
Row 2 Knit.
Row 3 K1, M1, K to last st, M1, K1. *6 sts*
Row 4 Knit.
Work in g st. Inc as set by row 3 on next
and 5 foll alt rows. *18 sts*
Cont in g st for a further 17 rows.
Place marker at each edge of last row.
Cont in g st for a further 32 rows.

Place marker at each edge of last row.
Cont in g st for a further 66 rows.
Next row K1, K2tog tbl, K to last 3 sts,
K2tog, K1. *16 sts*
Cont in g st for a further 5 rows.
Dec as set on next and foll 6th row. *12 sts*
Next row Knit.
Cont in yarn A only.

BASE
Beg with K row, work 18 rows in st st.
Next row K1, K2tog tbl, K to last 3 sts,
K2tog, K1. *10 sts*
Beg with P row, work 3 rows in st st.
Next row K1, K2tog tbl, K to last 3 sts,
K2tog, K1. *8 sts*
Next row Purl.

FEET
Cast on 18 sts at beg of next 2 rows. *44 sts*
Next row K1, M1, K16, K2tog tbl, K6, K2tog,
K16, M1, K1. *44 sts*
Next row Purl.
Next row K18, K2tog tbl, K4, K2tog, K18. *42 sts*
Next row Purl.
Next row K18, K2tog tbl, K2, K2tog, K18. *40 sts*
Beg with P row, work 5 rows in st st.
Next row K1, K2tog tbl, K to last 3 sts,
K2tog, K1. *38 sts*
Next row Purl.
Next row K1, K2tog tbl, K to last 3 sts,
K2tog, K1. *36 sts*
Next row Purl.

LEGS
Cast off 7 sts at beg of next 2 rows. *22 sts*
Beg with K row, work 12 rows in st st.
Next row K1, K2tog tbl, K to last 3 sts,
K2tog, K1. *20 sts*

Beg with P row, work 3 rows in st st.
Next row K1, K2tog tbl, K to last 3 sts,
K2tog, K1. *18 sts*
Next row Purl.
Next row K1, K2tog tbl, K5, M1, K2, M1, K5,
K2tog, K1. *18 sts*
Next row Purl.
Next row K1, K2tog tbl, K4, M1, K4, M1, K4,
K2tog, K1. *18 sts*
Next row Purl.
Cast off 4 sts at beg of next 2 rows. *10 sts*

TUMMY
Beg with K row, work 8 rows in st st.

ARMS
Cast on 6 sts at beg of next 2 rows. *22 sts*
Next row K1, M1, K5, M1, K10, M1, K5, M1,
K1. *26 sts*
Next row Purl.
Next row K1, M1, K7, M1, K10, M1, K7, M1,
K1. *30 sts*
Next row Purl.
Next row K10, M1, K10, M1, K10. *32 sts*
Next row Purl.
Next row K11, M1, K10, M1, K11. *34 sts*
Next row Purl.
Next row K1, K2tog tbl, K9, M1, K10, M1, K9,
K2tog, K1. *34 sts*
Next row Purl.
Next row K1, K2tog tbl, K9, M1, K10, M1, K9,
K2tog, K1. *34 sts*
Next row Purl.
Cast off 13 sts at beg of next 2 rows. *8 sts*

NECK/CHIN
Beg with K row, work 12 rows in st st.
Next row K1, K2tog tbl, K to last 3 sts,
K2tog, K1. *6 sts*

Beg with P row, work 7 rows in st st.
Next row K1, K2tog tbl, K2tog, K1. *4 sts*
Next row Purl.
Cast off.

BACK SECTION
Using 3.75mm (US 5) needles and yarns A and B held together cast on 4 sts.

TAIL
Row 1 Knit.
Row 2 Knit.
Row 3 K1, M1, K to last st, M1, K1. *6 sts*
Row 4 Knit.
Work in g st. Inc as set by row 3 on next and 5 foll alt rows. *18 sts*
Cont in g st for a further 49 rows.
Place marker at each edge of last row.
Cont in g st for a further 64 rows.
Place marker at each edge of last row.
Cont in g st for a further 30 rows.
Next row K1, K2tog tbl, K to last 3 sts, K2tog, K1. *16 sts*
Cont in g st for a further 3 rows.
Dec as set on next and foll 4th row. *12 sts*
Cont in g st for a further 11 rows.
Cont in yarn A only.
Cast on 28 sts at beg of next 2 rows. *68 sts*
Place markers on cast on edge, on 18th st from each edge, to denote the back of feet.

FEET
Next row K1, M1, K to last st, M1, K1. *70 sts*
Beg with P row, work 9 rows in st st.
Next row K1, K2tog tbl, K to last 3 sts, K2tog, K1. *68 sts*
Next row Purl.
Next row K1, K2tog tbl, K to last 3 sts, K2tog, K1. *66 sts*
Next row Purl.

LEGS
Cast off 7 sts at beg of next 2 rows. 52 sts
Next row K20, M1, K12, M1, K20. 54 sts
Beg with P row, work 11 rows in st st.
Next row K1, K2tog tbl, K to last 3 sts, K2tog, K1. 52 sts
Beg with P row, work 3 rows in st st.
Next row K1, K2tog tbl, K to last 3 sts,

K2tog, K1. *50 sts*
Next row Purl.
Next row K1, K2tog tbl, K to last 3 sts, K2tog, K1. *48 sts*
Next row Purl.
Next row K1, K2tog tbl, K13, K2tog tbl, K12, K2tog, K13, K2tog, K1. *44 sts*
Next row Purl.
Cast off 5 sts at beg of next 2 rows. *34 sts*

BACK

Next row K10, K2tog tbl, K10, K2tog, K10. *32 sts*
Next row Purl.
Next row K10, K2tog tbl, K8, K2tog, K10. *30sts*
Beg with P row, work 5 rows in st st.

ARMS

Cast on 6 sts at beg of next 2 rows. *42 sts*
Next row K1, M1, K5, M1, K10, K2tog tbl, K6, K2tog, K10, M1, K5, M1, K1. *44 sts*
Next row Purl.
Next row K1, M1, K7, M1, K28, M1, K7, M1, K1. *48 sts*
Next row Purl.
Next row K10, M1, K28, M1, K10. *50 sts*
Next row Purl.
Next row K11, M1, K10, K2tog tbl, K4, K2tog, K10, M1, K11. *50 sts*
Next row Purl.
Next row K1, K2tog tbl, K9, M1, K26, M1, K9, K2tog, K1. *50 sts*
Next row Purl.
Next row K1, K2tog tbl, K9, M1, K26, M1, K9, K2tog, K1. *50 sts*
Next row Purl.
Cast off 13 sts at beg of next 2 rows. *24 sts*

HEAD

Cast on 8 sts at beg of next 2 rows. *40 sts*
Next row K1, M1, K14, K2tog tbl, K6, K2tog, K14, M1, K1. *40 sts*
Next row Purl.
Next row K1, M1, K15, M1, K8, M1, K15, M1, K1. *44 sts*
Next row Purl.
Next row K1, M1, K to last st, M1, K1. *46 sts*
Next row Purl.
Place markers at each end of last row.
Next row K1, K2tog tbl, K16, M1, K8, M1, K16, K2tog, K1. *46 sts*
Next row Purl.

Next row K1, K2tog tbl, K16, M1, K8, M1, K16, K2tog, K1. *46 sts*
Next row Purl.
Next row K1, K2tog tbl, K to last 3 sts, K2tog, K1. *44 sts*
Next row Purl.
Next row K1, K2tog tbl, K to last 3 sts, K2tog, K1. *42 sts*
Next row Purl.
Cast off 16 sts at beg of next 2 rows. *10 sts*
Next row K1, M1, K to last st, M1, K1. *12 sts*
Beg with P row, work 3 rows in st st.
Next row K1, M1, K to last st, M1, K1. *14 sts*
Beg with P row, work 15 rows in st st.
Place marker at each end of last row to denote beg of face shaping.
Next row K1, K2tog tbl, K to last 3 sts, K2tog, K1. *12 sts*
Beg with P row, work 3 rows in st st.
Next row K1, K2tog tbl, K to last 3 sts, K2tog, K1. *10 sts*
Beg with P row, work 3 rows in st st.
Next row K1, K2tog tbl, K to last 3 sts, K2tog, K1. *8 sts*
Next row Purl.

Next row K1, K2tog tbl, K to last 3 sts, K2tog, K1. *6 sts*
Next row Purl.
Next row K1, K2tog tbl, K to last 3 sts, K2tog, K1. *4 sts*
Next row Purl.
Cast off.

EARS (BOTH ALIKE)
Using 3.75mm (US 5) needles and yarns A and B held together cast on 9 sts.

Row 1 Knit.
Row 2 Knit.
Row 3 K2tog tbl, K to last 2 sts, K2tog. 7 sts
Work in g st. Dec as set by row 3 on 2 foll 4th rows. *3 sts*
Next row Knit.
Next row Sl1, K2tog, PSSO.
Fasten off.

SCARF
Using 3.75mm (US 5) needles and yarn C cast on 6 sts.

Row 1 Knit.
Rep this row until scarf measures approx. 40cm (16in).
Cast off.

MAKING UP
Using mattress stitch, join top section of head to sides of head, matching markers on the top section of head to the cast off edge of head sides, and the cast off edge of top section to markers on head sides.

Matching arms, legs and markers on back section to back of feet on front section – join front and back sections, leaving base and tail open.

Stuff firmly.

Join base evenly along cast on edges of back section.

Join top and bottom sections of tail – matching markers to create curve and stuffing as you go along. Secure tail to back of squirrel approx. 18cm (7in) up from base.

Using dark brown yarn, embroider eyes and nose on face.

Sew ears in position on head, using image as a guide.

GINGER
BLANKET

This blanket has a cheerful jade background with contrasting tweedy squirrel silhouettes. Ginger blanket is knitted in panels for ease, and has two size options.

MATERIALS

YARN
Rowan Baby Merino Silk DK

		Small	Large
A	Emerald 685	3 × 50g	6 × 50g

Rowan Felted Tweed

B	Ginger 154	2 × 50g	4 × 50g

NEEDLES
1 pair 4mm (no 8) (US 6) needles

TENSION
22 sts and 30 rows to 10cm (4in) measured over st st using 4mm (US 6) needles.

FINISHED SIZE
Small baby blanket measures approx. 55 × 60cm (21¾ × 23¾in).

Large baby blanket measures approx. 80 × 90cm (31½ × 35½in).

SMALL BABY BLANKET
PANEL A (MAKE 2)
Using yarn A and 4mm (US 6) needles cast on 29 sts.

Working in st st throughout, starting with a K row and using the intarsia technique, work from chart A (page 64) until all 84 rows have been completed twice. Cast off.

PANEL B (MAKE 2)
Using yarn A and 4mm (US 6) needles cast on 29 sts.

Working in st st throughout, starting with a K row and using the intarsia technique, work from chart B (page 65) until all 84 rows have been completed twice.
Cast off.

SIDE BORDERS (BOTH ALIKE)
Using yarn A and 4mm (US 6) needles cast on 1 st.

*Row 1 Inc 1 st. *2 sts*
Row 2 Knit.
Row 3 Knit.
Row 4 Knit.
Row 5 K1, M1, K to end. *3 sts*
Row 6 Knit.
Row 7 K1, M1, K to end. *4 sts*
Row 8 Knit.
Row 9 K1, M1, K to end. *5 sts*
Row 10 Knit.
Row 11 K1, M1, K to end. *6 sts*
Row 12 Knit.
Row 13 K1, M1, K to end. *7 sts*
Row 14 (WS) Knit.
Place marker at end of last row.**
Cont in g st until border measures the length of blanket from marker ending with RS facing for Next row.
***Next row Place marker at beg of row, K to end.
Next row K to last 2 sts, K2tog. *6 sts*
Next row Knit.
Next row K to last 2 sts, K2tog. *5 sts*
Next row Knit.
Next row K to last 2 sts, K2tog. *4 sts*
Next row Knit.
Next row K to last 2 sts, K2tog. *3 sts*
Next row Knit.
Next row K to last 2 sts, K2tog. *2 sts*
Next row Knit.

Next row Knit.
Next row Knit.
Next row K2tog.
Fasten off.

TOP & BOTTOM BORDERS (BOTH ALIKE)
Using yarn A and 4mm (US 6) needles cast on 1 st.

Work as side borders from * to **
Cont in g st until border measures the width of blanket from marker ending with RS facing for next row.
Complete as side borders from ***

LARGE BABY BLANKET
PANEL A (MAKE 3)
Using yarn A and 4mm (US 6) needles cast on 29 sts.

Working in st st throughout, starting with a K row and using the intarsia technique, work from chart A until all 84 rows have been completed 3 times.
Cast off.

PANEL B (MAKE 3)
Using yarn A and 4mm (US 6) needles cast on 29 sts.

Working in st st throughout, starting with a K row and using the intarsia technique, work from chart B until all 84 rows have been completed 3 times.
Cast off.

SIDE BORDERS (BOTH ALIKE)

Using yarn A and 4mm (US 6) needles cast on 1 st.

*__Row 1__ Inc 1 st. *2 sts*
__Row 2__ Knit.
__Row 3__ Knit.
__Row 4__ Knit.
__Row 5__ K1, M1, K to end. *3 sts*
__Row 6__ Knit.
__Row 7__ K1, M1, K to end. *4 sts*
__Row 8__ Knit.
__Row 9__ K1, M1, K to end. *5 sts*
__Row 10__ Knit.
__Row 11__ K1, M1, K to end. *6 sts*
__Row 12__ Knit.
__Row 13__ K1, M1, K to end. *7 sts*
__Row 14 (WS)__ Knit.
Place marker at end of last row.**
Cont in g st until border measures the length of blanket from marker ending with RS facing for next row.
***__Next row__ Place marker at beg of row, K to end.
__Next row__ K to last 2 sts, K2tog. *6 sts*
__Next row__ Knit.
__Next row__ K to last 2 sts, K2tog. *5 sts*
__Next row__ Knit.
__Next row__ K to last 2 sts, K2tog. *4 sts*
__Next row__ Knit.
__Next row__ K to last 2 sts, K2tog. *3 sts*
__Next row__ Knit.
__Next row__ K to last 2 sts, K2tog. *2 sts*
__Next row__ Knit.
__Next row__ Knit.
__Next row__ Knit.
__Next row__ K2tog.
Fasten off.

TOP & BOTTOM BORDERS (BOTH ALIKE)

Using yarn A and 4mm (US 6) needles cast on 1 st.

Work as side borders from * to **
Cont in g st until border measures the width of blanket from marker ending with RS facing for next row.
Complete as side borders from ***

MAKING UP

Using mattress st, join blanket panels following the layout plan.

With shorter edges facing blanket – sew top, bottom and side borders to blanket between markers.

Join border corners using mattress st.

LARGE BABY BLANKET LAYOUT PLAN

Panel A	Panel B	Panel A	Panel B	Panel A	Panel B

SMALL BABY BLANKET LAYOUT PLAN

Panel A	Panel B	Panel A	Panel B

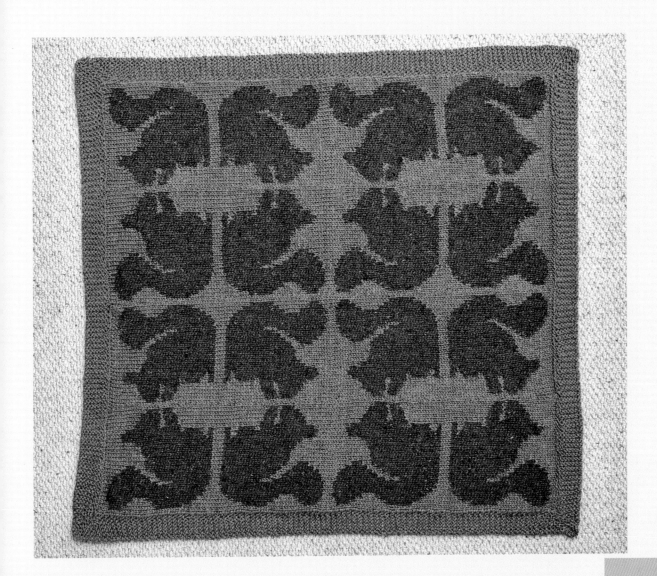

KEY

Yarn A

Yarn B

ROW I

CHART B

Yarn A
Yarn B

ROW I

POM POM BUNTING

This bunting matches Bertie and Bea's fluffy tails perfectly. A really simple project and a great way to use up any oddments leftover from other projects in this book!

MATERIALS

YARN

Rowan Baby Merino Silk DK

A	Claret	700	1 × 50g
B	Iceberg	699	1 × 50g
C	Zinc	681	1 × 50g
D	Rose	678	1 × 50g
E	Emerald	685	1 × 50g
F	Dawn	672	1 × 50g

EXTRAS

Approx. 4m × 3mm double satin light grey ribbon

35mm (1⅜in) pom pom maker

FINISHED SIZE

Completed bunting measures approx. 140cm (55⅛in) long from first pom pom to last pom pom.

POM POM BUNTING

Using 35mm (1⅜in) pom pom maker and yarn A create a pom pom and secure it using the ribbon, leaving approx. 30cm (11¾in) of ribbon before 1st pom pom.

Using 35mm (1⅜in) pom pom maker and yarn B create a pom pom and secure it using the ribbon, leaving approx. 6cm of ribbon between pom poms.

Using 35mm (1⅜in) pom pom maker and yarn C create a pom pom and secure it using the ribbon, leaving approx. 6cm (2¼in) of ribbon between pom poms.

Using 35mm (1⅜in) pom pom maker and yarn D create a pom pom and secure it using the ribbon, leaving approx. 6cm (2¼in) of ribbon between pom poms.

Using 35mm (1⅜in) pom pom maker and yarn E create a pom pom and secure it

using the ribbon, leaving approx. 6cm (2¼in)
of ribbon between pom poms.

Using 35mm (1⅜in) pom pom maker and
yarn F create a pom pom and secure it using
the ribbon, leaving approx. 6cm (2¼in) of
ribbon between pom poms.

Cont adding pom poms in this order until
there are 6 of each shade on bunting
(or until required length).

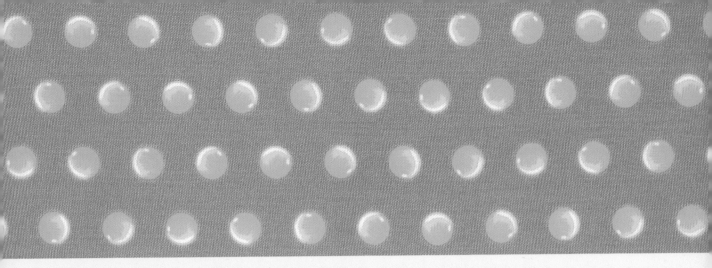

SLEEPY OWL PILLOW

This nocturnal sleepy owl is knitted using a combination of fair-isle and intarsia and will keep you comfy in your nursing chair, day or night.

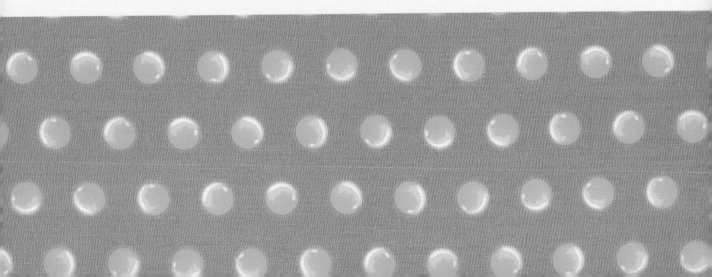

MATERIALS

YARN

Rowan Pure Wool Superwash DK

A	Shale	002	2 x 50g
B	Anthracite	003	1 x 50g
C	Raspberry	028	1 x 50g
D	Avacado	019	1 x 50g
E	Gold	051	1 x 50g

FABRIC

29 x 50cm (11½ x 19¾in) piece of Tula Pink Pearls of Wisdom fabric in tartx, cut to size using pinking shears

40 x 50cm (16 x 19¾in) piece of Tula Pink Pearls of Wisdom fabric in tartx, cut to size using pinking shears

NEEDLES

1 pair 4mm (no 8) (US 6) needles

EXTRAS

46cm (18in) square pillow pad

TENSION

22 sts and 30 rows to 10cm (4in) measured over st st using 4mm (US 6) needles.

FINISHED SIZE

Knitted pillow panel measures approx. 46cm (18in) square.

FRONT

Using yarn A and 4mm (US 6) needles cast on 103 sts.
Beg with k row, work in st st for 38 rows, ending with a WS row.
Next row Working as set on row 1 of chart and using the intarsia technique, work 88 sts from chart, K15.
Next row P15, working as set on row 2 of chart and using the intarsia technique, work 88 sts from chart (page 74).
These 2 rows set chart placement.
Cont as set on chart (page 74), using the intarsia and fair-isle techniques (fair-isle for owl's tummy only) until all 78 rows have been completed, ending with RS facing for next row. Cont in st st using yarn A only until front meas 46cm (18in), ending with a WS row.
Cast off.

MAKING UP

Pillow cover back: For opening edges, turn under 2cm (¾in) along one long edge of each piece. Turn under again and straight stitch in place. With RS of knitting facing RS of fabric, place smaller piece on the knitted front first, place the larger piece on top, overlapping in the middle.

Pin and handstitch the sides of the two pieces to the knitted front.

Turn the right sides out and insert pillow pad.

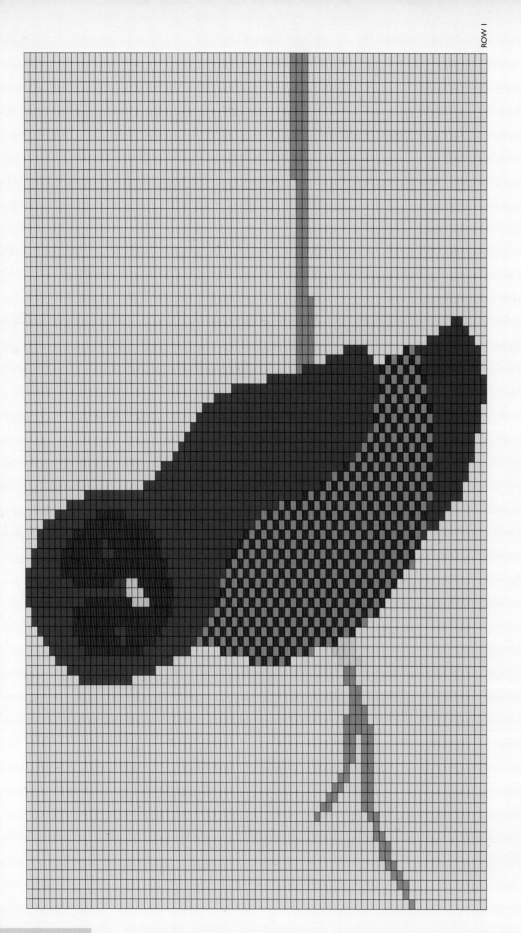

KEY

☐ Yarn A
■ Yarn B
■ Yarn C
■ Yarn D
☐ Yarn E

OLLIE AND POLLY ELEPHANT

These baby elephants are super cute and cuddly.
Their colourful tails, foot pads and stripey ears will brighten
up any nursery.

MATERIALS

YARN
Rowan Cotton Glace

OLLIE
A	Dawn Grey	831	2 x 50g
B	Mineral	856	1 x 50g
C	Winsor	849	1 x 50g
D	Shoot	814	1 x 50g

POLLY
A	Dawn Grey	831	2 x 50g
B	Lipstick	865	1 x 50g
C	Persimmon	832	1 x 50g
D	Poppy	741	1 x 50g

NEEDLES
1 pair 3.25mm (no 10) (US 3) needles

EXTRAS
Washable toy stuffing
Small crochet hook (3mm to 3.75mm)

TENSION
23 sts and 32 rows to 10cm (4in)
measured over st st using 3.25mm
(US 3) needles.

FINISHED SIZE
Both Ollie and Polly measure approx. 25cm
(10in) long, 10.5cm (4¼in) wide across back
and 17.5cm (7in) tall.

TOP SECTION
Using 3.25mm (US 3) needles and yarn A
cast on 2 sts.

TAIL
Row 1 Knit.
Row 2 Purl.
Row 3 K1, M1, K1. *3 sts*
Beg with P row, work 3 rows in st st.
Next row K1, M1, K2. *4 sts*
Beg with P row, work 5 rows in st st.
Next row K1, M1, K to last st, M1, K1. *6 sts*
Inc as set on 3 foll 6th rows. *12 sts*
Beg with P row, work 3 rows in st st.

BACK LEGS
Cast on 33 sts at beg of next 2 rows.
Place a marker on 11th st from each edge
along cast on edge to denote top of legs. *78 sts*

Next row K33, M1, K12, M1, K to end. *80 sts*
Next row Purl.
Next row K33, M1 K14, M1, K to end. *82 sts*
Beg with P row, work 13 rows in st st.
Cast off 11 sts at beg of next 2 rows. *60 sts*
Beg with K row, work 14 rows in st st.

FRONT LEGS
Cast on 11 sts at beg of next 2 rows. *82 sts*
Beg with K row, work 14 rows in st st.
Next row K29, K2tog tbl, K20, K2tog, K to end. *80 sts*
Next row Purl.
Cast off 30 sts at beg of next 2 rows. *20 sts*
Place markers at each end of last row.

HEAD
Beg with K row, work 12 rows in st st.
Next row K1, K2tog tbl, K to last 3 sts, K2tog, K1. *18 sts*
Beg with P row, work 3 rows in st st.
Next row K1, K2tog tbl, K to last 3 sts, K2tog, K1. *16 sts*
Next row Purl.
Break of yarn.
With RS facing, pick up and knit 18 sts from right side of work, between stitch marker and needle, knit 16 sts from needle, then pick up and knit 18 sts along left side of work to second stitch marker. *52 sts*
Beg with P row, work 11 rows in st st.
Next row K14, K2tog tbl, K20, K2tog, K14. *50 sts*
Next row Purl.
Next row K13, K2tog tbl, K20, K2tog, K13. *48 sts*
Next row Purl.
Next row K12, K2tog tbl, K20, K2tog, K12. *46 sts*
Next row P11, P2tog, P20, P2tog tbl, P11. *44 sts*
Next row K10, K2tog tbl, K20, K2tog, K10. *42 sts*
Next row P9, P2tog, P20, P2tog tbl, P9. *40 sts*
Next row K8, K2tog tbl, K20, K2tog, K8. *38 sts*

Next row P7, P2tog, P20, P2tog tbl, P7. *36 sts*
Next row K6, K2tog tbl, K20, K2tog, K6. *34 sts*
Next row P5, P2tog, P20, P2tog tbl, P5. *32 sts*
Next row K4, K2tog tbl, K20, K2tog, K4. *30 sts*
Next row P3, P2tog, P20, P2tog tbl, P3. *28 sts*
Next row K2, K2tog tbl, K20, K2tog, K2. *26 sts*
Next row P1, P2tog, P20, P2tog tbl, P1. *24 sts*
Next row K1, K2tog tbl, K18, K2tog, K1 *22 sts*
Next row Purl.
Next row K1, K2tog tbl, K16, K2tog, K1. *20 sts*

TRUNK
Next row (WS) Knit.
Next row K1, K2tog tbl, K to last 3 sts, K2tog, K1. *18 sts*
Next row Purl.
Next row K1, K2tog tbl, K to last 3 sts, K2tog, K1. *16 sts*
Next row Purl.
Next row K1, K2tog tbl, K to last 3 sts, K2tog, K1. *14 sts*
Next row Purl.
Next row K1, K2tog tbl, K to last 3 sts, K2tog, K1. *12 sts*
Next row (WS) Knit.
Next row K1, K2tog tbl, K to last 3 sts, K2tog, K1. *10 sts*
Next row Purl.
Next row Knit.
Next row Purl.
Next row K1, K2tog tbl, K to last 3 sts, K2tog, K1. *8 sts*
Next row Purl.
Next row Knit.
Next row (WS) Knit.
Beg with K row, work 7 rows in st st.
Next row (WS) Knit.
Rep last 8 rows once more.
Beg with K row, work 9 rows in st st.
Next row (WS) Knit.

Next row Knit.
Next row Purl.
Next row K2tog tbl, K to last 2 sts, K2tog. *6 sts*
Next row Purl.
Next row Knit.
Next row Purl.
Next row K2tog tbl, K to last 2 sts, K2tog. *4 sts*
Cast off Pwise.

BOTTOM SECTION
Using 3.25mm (US 3) needles and yarn A cast on 10 sts.

Row 1 Knit.
Row 2 Purl.
Row 3 K1, M1, K to last st, M1, K1. *12 sts*
Row 4 Purl.
Row 5 K1, M1, K to last st, M1, K1. *14 sts*
Row 6 Purl.
Row 7 K1, M1, K to last st, M1, K1. *16 sts*
Beg with P row, work 19 rows in st st.
Place marker at each end of last row.

BACK LEGS
Cast on 11 sts at beg of next 2 rows. *38 sts*
*****Next row** K10, K2tog tbl, K14, K2tog, K10. *36 sts*
Next row Purl.
Next row K10, K2tog tbl, K12, K2tog, K10. *34 sts*
Next row Purl.
Next row K10, K2tog tbl, K10, K2tog, K10. *32 sts*
Beg with P row, work 3 rows in st st.
Next row K11, M1, K10, M1, K11. *34 sts*
Next row Purl.
Next row K11, M1, K12, M1, K11. *36 sts*
Next row Purl.
Next row K11, M1, K14, M1, K11. *38 sts*

Next row Purl.**
Cast off 11 sts at beg of next 2 rows. *16 sts*
Beg with K row, work 14 rows in st st.

FRONT LEGS
Cast on 11 sts at beg of next 2 rows. *38 sts*
Work as back legs from * to **
Cast off 11 sts at beg of next 2 rows. *16 sts*
Beg with K row, work 20 rows in st st.
Place markers at each end of last row, to denote start of head.

HEAD
Beg with K row, work 29 rows in st st.

TRUNK
Next row (WS) Knit.
Next row K1, K2tog tbl, K to last 3 sts, K2tog, K1. *14 sts*

Next row Purl.
Next row K1, K2tog tbl, K to last 3 sts, K2tog, K1. *12 sts*
Next row Purl.
Next row K1, K2tog tbl, K to last 3 sts, K2tog, K1. *10 sts*
Next row (WS) Knit.
Next row Knit.
Next row Purl.
Next row K1, K2tog tbl, K to last 3 sts, K2tog, K1. *8 sts*
Next row Purl.
Next row Knit.
Next row (WS) Knit.
Beg with K row, work 5 rows in st st.
Next row (WS) Knit.
Rep last 6 rows 2 times more.
Next row Knit.
Next row Purl.
Next row K2tog tbl, K to last 2 sts, K2tog. *6 sts*
Next row Purl.
Next row K2tog tbl, K to last 2 sts, K2tog. *4 sts*
Cast off Pwise.

EARS (MAKE 2)
Using 3.25mm (US 3) needles and yarn C cast on 11 sts.
Row 1 Knit.
Row 2 K1, M1, K to last st, M1, K1. *13 sts*
Row 3 Knit.
Change to yarn B
Row 4 K1, M1, K to last st, M1, K1. *15 sts*
Row 5 Knit.
Row 6 K1, M1, K to last st, M1, K1. *17 sts*
Row 7 Knit.
Change to yarn A
Row 8 K1, M1, K to last st, M1, K1. *19 sts*
Row 9 Knit.
Row 10 K1, M1, K to last st, M1, K1. *21 sts*
Row 11 Knit.

Change to yarn D
Row 12 K1, M1, K to last st, M1, K1. *23 sts*
Row 13 Knit.
Row 14 K1, M1, K to last st, M1, K1. *25 sts*
Row 15 Knit.
Change to yarn C
Knit 4 rows.
Change to yarn B
Knit 4 rows.
Change to yarn A
Next row K1, K2tog tbl, K to last 3 sts, K2tog, K1. *23 sts*
Next row Knit.
Next row K1, K2tog tbl, K to last 3 sts, K2tog, K1. *21 sts*
Next row Knit.
Change to yarn D

Next row K1, K2tog tbl, K to last 3 sts, K2tog, K1. *19 sts*
Next row Knit.
Next row K1, K2tog tbl, K to last 3 sts, K2tog, K1. *17 sts*
Next row K1, K2tog tbl, K to last 3 sts, K2tog, K1. *15 sts*
Cast off.

FOOT PADS (MAKE 1 EACH IN YARN A, B, C AND D)
Using 3.25mm (US 3) needles cast on 6 sts.

Row 1 Knit.
Row 2 K1, M1, K to last st, M1, K1. *8 sts*
Row 3 Knit.
Row 4 K1, M1, K to last st, M1, K1. *10 sts*
Knit 9 rows.
Next row K1, K2tog tbl, K to last 3 sts, K2tog, K1. *8 sts*
Next row Knit.
Next row K1, K2tog tbl, K to last 3 sts, K2tog, K1. *6 sts*
Cast off.

MAKING UP
Matching markers and using mattress stitch, join top and bottom sections along cast off edges of right front leg, under the chin, around trunk (matching WS knit rows to create curve), along the left seam of chin and across cast off edges of left leg, stuffing as you go.

Join top and bottom sections along back seams of front legs (leaving foot open for foot pads), along underbelly and down the front seams of back legs, stuffing as you go.

Matching markers, join back seams of back legs and bottom section of elephant.

Sew foot pads in place.

Using yarn C, embroider eyes on face.

Sew ears in position on head, using image as a guide.

TAIL TASSEL
Cut 7 strands of yarn C, approx. 15cm (6in) long.

Loop the centre of these strands through the cast on end of tail using a crochet hook and pull both ends of strands through the centre of loop, pulling tight.

Trim to required length.

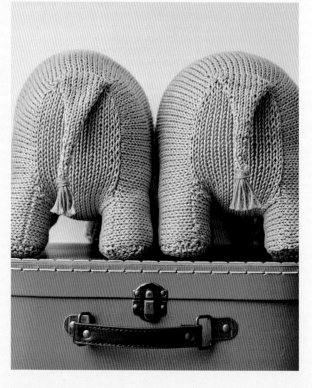

OLLIE AND POLLY BLANKETS

These very simple striped blankets are the perfect project for a complete beginner. They coordinate with Ollie and Polly Elephant and are a great size for the pram or a Moses basket.

MATERIALS

YARN
Rowan Cotton Glace

OLLIE BLANKET
A	Winsor	849	2 × 50g
B	Mineral	856	2 × 50g
C	Dawn Grey	831	2 × 50g
D	Shoot	814	2 × 50g

POLLY BLANKET
A	Persimmon	832	2 × 50g
B	Lipstick	865	2 × 50g
C	Dawn Grey	831	2 × 50g
D	Poppy	741	2 × 50g

NEEDLES
1 pair 3.75mm (no 9) (US 5) needles

TENSION
22 sts and 43 rows to 10cm (4in) measured over garter st using 3.75mm (US 5) needles.

FINISHED SIZE
Both Ollie and Polly blankets measure approx. 63cm (25in) wide and 65cm (25½in) long.

BLANKET
Using 3.75mm (US 5) needles and yarn A cast on 138 sts.

Rows 1 to 10 Knit.
Change to yarn B
Rows 11 to 20 Knit.
Change to yarn C
Rows 21 to 30 Knit.
Change to yarn D
Rows 31 to 40 Knit.
Rep these 40 rows 6 times further.
Cast off.

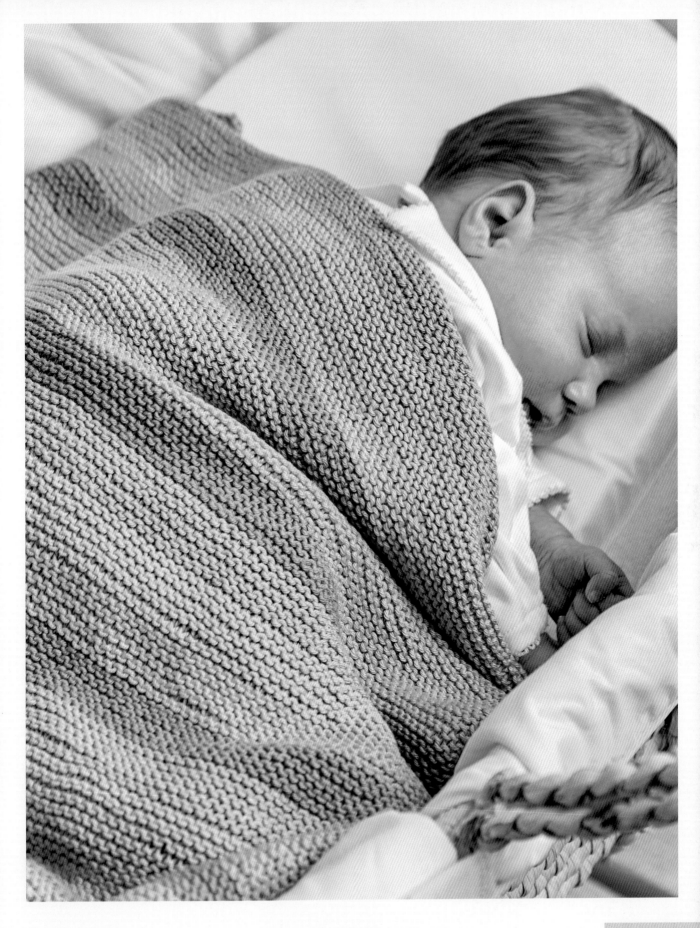

CIRCULAR FELTED RUG

This simple rug is knitted and felted in the washing machine to create a lovely hardwearing surface – perfect for rest and play in the home or even a shady spot of the garden.

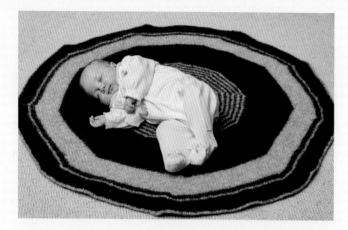

MATERIALS

YARN
Rowan Creative Focus Worsted

A	Nickel	0401	2 x 100g
B	Syrah	2025	3 x 100g

NEEDLES
5.5mm (no 5) (US 9) circular needle

TENSION
Before felting: 17 sts and 23 rows to 10cm (4in) measured over st st using 5.5mm (US 9) needle.

After felting: 22 sts and 30 rows to 10cm (4in) measured over st st using 5.5mm (US 9) needle.

FINISHED SIZE
Completed rug measures approx. 88cm (34¾in) in diameter.

SPECIAL ABBREIVIATIONS
Kfb – Inc 1 st by knitting into the front and back of next st.

PLAYMAT
Using yarn A and 5.5mm (US 9) needle cast on 3 sts.

Row 1 *Kfb, rep from * to end. *6 sts*
Change to yarn B
Row 2 Purl.
Row 3 K1, *Kfb, rep from * to last st, K1. *10 sts*
Change to yarn A
Row 4 Purl.
Row 5 K1, *Kfb, rep from * to end. *19 sts*
Change to yarn B

Row 6 Purl.
Row 7 K1, *Kfb, K1, rep from * to end. *28 sts*
Change to yarn A
Row 8 Purl.
Row 9 K1, *Kfb, K2, rep from * to end. *37 sts*
Change to yarn B
Row 10 Purl.
Row 11 K1, *Kfb, K3, rep from * to end. *46 sts*
Change to yarn A
Row 12 Purl.
Row 13 K1, *Kfb, K4, rep from * to end. *55 sts*
Rows 4 to 13 set pattern, increasing 1 st per
'section' on each alt row.
Cont in patt for 44 rows more, changing
yarn every 2 rows. *253 sts*
Change to yarn B
Cont in patt for a further 36 rows. *415 sts*
Change to yarn A
Cont in patt for a further 20 rows. *505 sts*
Change to yarn B
Cont in patt for a further 4 rows. *523 sts*
Change to yarn A
Cont in patt for a further 2 rows. *532 sts*
Change to yarn B
Cont in patt for a further 12 rows. *586 sts*
Next row (WS) Knit
Change to yarn A
Next row K1, *Kfb, K64, rep from * to end.
595 sts
Cast off.

MAKING UP

Sew seam together and sew in all ends.
Wash in the machine on its own at 30°C.
Pull into shape and flatten whilst damp, then
dry flat.

ABBREVIATIONS

alt	alternate	P2tog	purl next 2 stitches together
approx.	approximately	rep	repeat
beg	begin(s)(ning)	RS	right side
cm	centimetres	sl 1	slip one stitch
cont	continu(e)(ing)	SSK	slip 2 sts to right hand needle
dec	decreas(e)(ing)		kwise, insert point of left needle
foll	follow(s)(ing)		into front of these 2 sts (from
g	gram		left to right), take yarn rnd
g st	garter stitch – knit every row		needle and take 2 sts off
in	inch(es)	st(s)	stitch(es)
inc	increas(e)(ing)	st st	stocking stitch/US stockinette
K	knit		stitch (1 row knit, 1 row purl)
K2tog	knit next 2 stitches together	tbl	through back of loop(s)
M1	make one stitch by picking	tog	together
	up horizontal loop before	WS	wrong side
	next stitch and knitting into	[ ]/*	repeat instructions within
	back of it		square brackets or
P	purl		between asterisks
psso	pass slipped stitch over		

Ginger
Squirrel

ACKNOWLEDGEMENTS

I'd like to say a huge thank you to Darren and Georgie at Quail for bringing this book to life! Jesse for his wonderful photography. Annette, Gary and Tash for letting us take over their house for a day, and beautiful Sophia-Rose for modelling.

Thank you to Steph, both for her knitting and ongoing support. Dawn, Gwynneth, Sharon and Emma for their lovely knitting. Marilyn for her thorough pattern checking. Rowan for providing the yarn for this book. And finally thanks to Andrew for looking after me when I was very busy!

For a complete list of all our books see
www.searchpress.com